AFGHANISTAN
the culture

Erinn Banting

A Bobbie Kalman Book

The Lands, Peoples, and Cultures Series

 Crabtree Publishing Company
www.crabtreebooks.com

The Lands, Peoples, and Cultures Series

Created by Bobbie Kalman

Coordinating editor
Ellen Rodger

Production coordinator
Rosie Gowsell

Project editor
Carrie Gleason

Project development, design, editing, and photo editing
First Folio Resource Group, Inc.
Erinn Banting
Tom Dart
Greg Duhaney
Jaimie Nathan
Debbie Smith

Photo research
Image Select International Ltd/UK

Prepress and printing
Worzalla Publishing Company

Consultants
S. Irtiza Hasan, Muslim Students Association at the University of Houston; Mohammad Masoom Hotak

Photographs
AFP/Corbis/Magma: title page, p. 12 (right), p. 15 (both), p. 16 (top), p. 17 (right), p. 19 (bottom), p. 29; Alamy/F. Jack Jackson: p. 19 (top); Paul Almasy/Corbis/Magma: p. 23 (top); AP Photo/Xinhua, Ainiwar: p. 16 (bottom); AP Photo/Gregory Bull: p. 11 (top); AP Photo/Kamran Jebreili: p. 26; AP Photo/Efrem Lukatsky: p. 7 (right); AP Photo/Maxim Marmur: p. 4 (bottom); AP Photo/Suzanne Plunkett: p. 27 (bottom); AP Photo/Hasan Sarbakhsian: p. 14; AP Photo/Lynne Sladky: p. 27 (top); Art Directors and TRIP: p. 22; Art Directors and TRIP/M. Barlow: p. 9; Baci/Corbis/Magma: p. 18 (top); Burstein Collection/Corbis/Magma: p. 28; Ric Ergenbright: cover, p. 8 (left), p. 21 (top); Ric Ergenbright/Corbis/Magma: p. 24 (left); Doranne Jacobson: p. 3; Charles and Josette Lenars/Corbis/Magma: p. 5; Quidu Noel/Gamma: p. 10; Aventurier Patrick/Gamma: p. 11 (bottom); Ben Rashid: p. 24 (right); Reuters NewMedia Inc./Corbis/Magma: p. 8 (right), p. 12 (left), p. 13 (both), p. 20 (right), p. 25; Rex Features: p. 18 (bottom); Jon Spaull/Corbis/

Magma: p. 21 (bottom); Sven/Corbis Sygma/Magma: p. 23 (bottom); Andrew Tompkins: p. 20 (left); Topham Picturepoint: p. 6; Venturi/Contrasto: p. 7 (left); Kontos Yannis/Gamma: p. 17 (left); Zaheeruddin/Corbis Sygma/Magma: p. 4 (top)

Illustrations
Dianne Eastman: icon
David Wysotski, Allure Illustrations: back cover
Alexei Mezentsev: pp. 30–31

Cover: The ruins of the Khaja Mohammed Parsa, a mosque that was built during the 1400s, still stand in Balkh, in northern Afghanistan.

Icon: A *rebab*, which appears at the head of each section, is a stringed instrument used in Afghan folk music.

Title page: Two friends chat outside the Eid-Gah Mosque in Kabul, Afghanistan's capital. They are at the mosque to celebrate the religious festival of *Eid ul-Fitar*.

Back cover: A dromedary is a type of camel with one hump. Camels have adapted to Afghanistan's harsh desert climate. They can survive on very little water, they have thick pads on their legs that allow them to kneel in the hot desert sand, and they can close their nostrils to avoid getting dust in their noses.

Published by
Crabtree Publishing Company

PMB 16A,	612 Welland Avenue	73 Lime Walk
350 Fifth Avenue	St. Catharines	Headington
Suite 3308	Ontario, Canada	Oxford OX3 7AD
New York	L2M 5V6	United Kingdom
N.Y. 10118		

Cataloging in Publication Data
Banting, Erinn.
  Afghanistan. The culture / Erinn Banting.
    p. cm. -- (Lands, peoples, cultures series)
  Includes index.
  ISBN 0-7787-9337-0 (RLB) -- ISBN 0-7787-9705-8 (PB)
  1. Afghanistan--Civilization--Juvenile literature. [1. Afghanistan--Civilization. 2. Afghanistan--Social life and customs.] I.
  Title. II. Series: Lands, peoples, and cultures series.
  DS354.B329 2003
  958.1--dc21
                                        2003001264
                                           LC

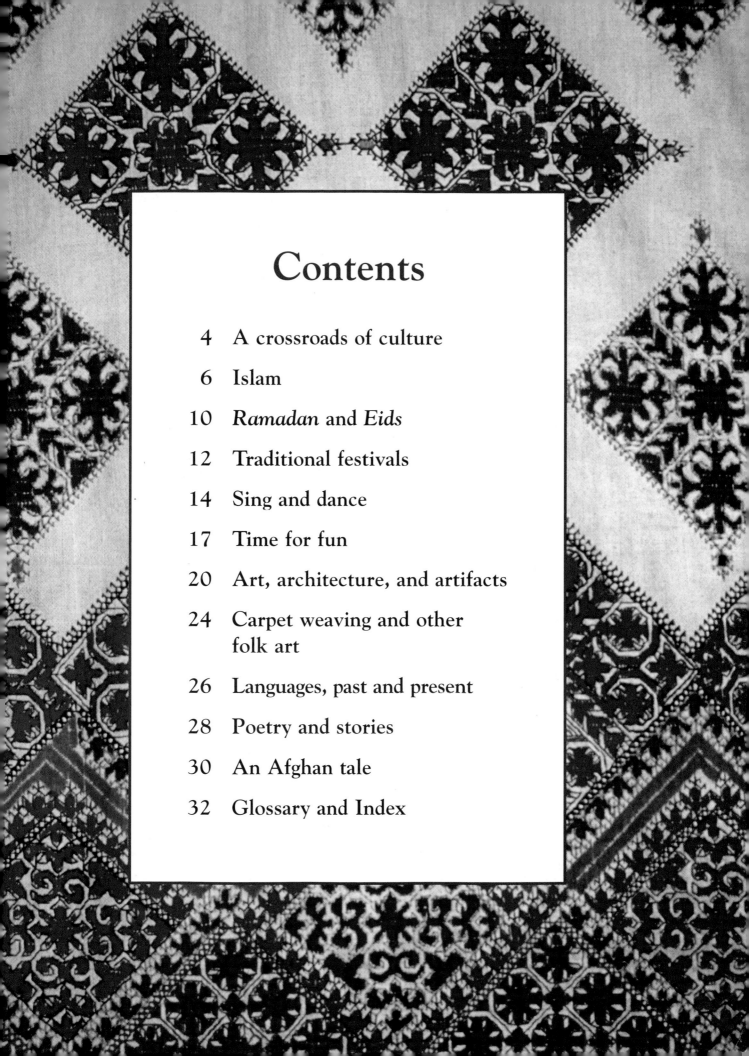

Contents

A crossroads of culture

Afghanistan is at the crossroads of the Middle East, Asia, and Europe. Its religion, art, music, and literature have been influenced by the people who moved there from surrounding countries, such as Tajikistan, Uzbekistan, Pakistan, and Iran. **Invaders** who forced their way through the land also influenced Afghanistan's culture. These invaders include the Persians, Macedonians, Arabs, Turks, Mongols, British, and Russians.

A threatened culture

Ancient **artifacts**, beautiful artwork and crafts, and poems and stories about love and history are evidence of Afghanistan's rich culture. Unfortunately, Afghanistan has also been the site of many wars, which have destroyed most of the country's elegant buildings. As well, many rulers have forbidden the people to practice their traditions. The Taliban, a religious and political movement that controlled much of Afghanistan from 1996 to 2001, did not allow people to celebrate non-religious festivals, listen to music, dance, or play games and sports. Anyone caught breaking the law was arrested, beaten, or put to death. Since the Taliban was removed from power, people have begun to celebrate their culture again.

(above) Afghan children learn to read in Pashto and Dari, the country's two main languages.

(opposite) Mosaic tiles arranged in different geometric and floral patterns decorate the Blue Mosque in Mazar-e-Sharif, a city in the north.

(below) Two boys enjoy a ride on a swing during Eid ul-Adha. The festival marks the end of a pilgrimage that many Muslims make to Mecca, a holy city in Saudi Arabia.

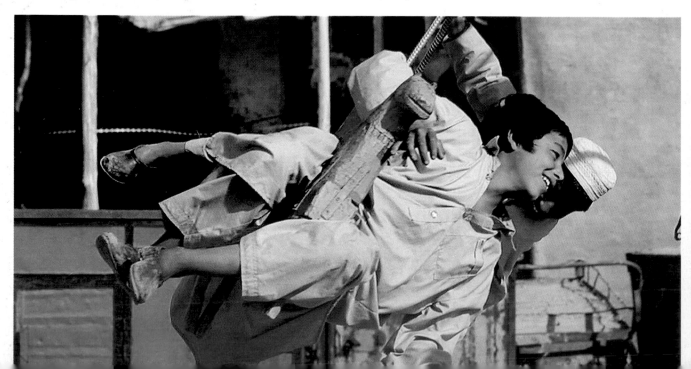

Islam

In the 700s, Arab invaders introduced the religion of Islam to Afghanistan. Today, almost 99 percent of Afghanistan's population is Muslim, or followers of Islam. Muslims believe in one god, Allah, and they follow the teachings of his **prophet** Muhammad. These teachings are recorded in the *Qur'an*, the Muslim holy book.

The Five Pillars of Islam

Muslims follow five principles known as the Five Pillars of Islam. The first principle is *shahadah*, or "bearing witness." This means that a person accepts Islam by saying, "There is no god but Allah and Muhammad is his prophet." The second principle is performing *salat*, or "prayer," five times a day. The third principle is called *sawm*, or **fasting** during the holy month of *Ramadan*. The fourth principle is going on *hajj* or a **pilgrimage** to Mecca. Mecca is the city in Saudi Arabia where the Ka' bah, Islam's most important **shrine**, is located. The final principle, *zakat*, encourages people to help others in the community, including giving to charity.

Prayer

Muslims pray five times a day — before sunrise, in the early afternoon, in the late afternoon, after sunset, and before going to bed. On Fridays, which is the Muslim Sabbath, or day of rest, special prayers are said during the early afternoon prayer time.

Every city and town in Afghanistan has a mosque. A muezzin, or prayer caller, summons people to worship at the mosque.

Hundreds of people pray in a market in Kabul during a Muslim holiday. Schools, workplaces, markets, and homes have areas where people can pray if they cannot go to a mosque.

Pilgrimages

Muslims who are healthy and have the money to do so are supposed to go on *hajj* to the holy city of Mecca. Within Afghanistan, people also go on pilgrimages to shrines that honor important religious figures, such as Muhammad; *mullahs*, or religious teachers; Afghan heroes; and poets. Some shrines are simple mounds of earth, while others are elaborately decorated tombs.

Women and children are the main visitors to shrines. They sometimes stay there for days at a time, paying their respects and asking for blessings. At some shrines, people buy **amulets** called *tawiz*, which are supposed to protect them from evil, bring good luck, and ensure wealth. Once a year, a large festival honors the person remembered at the shrine. The festival usually takes place on the anniversary of the person's death.

Sects of Islam

There are two main sects, or groups, of Muslims: Sunnis and Shias, or Shi'ites. These groups developed because people had different ideas about who should lead Islam after Muhammad's death. Sunnis believed Muhammad's **successor** should be elected. Shias believed that Muhammad chose his successor, his son-in-law and cousin Ali, and that future successors should be Ali's **descendants**. One group of Shias, the Ismailis, follow a spiritual leader called the Aga Khan. The Aga Khan also runs a charitable foundation that helps build irrigation systems, hospitals, schools, and **mosques** around the word. Other differences separate Sunnis and Shias, including the fact that they follow different *Sunnah*, or customs, and *Hadiths*, or records of Muhammad's words and actions.

Shia Muslims pray at the Blue Mosque in Mazar-e-Sharif. About 20 percent of Afghans are Shia.

Sufism

Sufism is the **mystical** side of Islam. Both Sunnis and Shias practice Sufism, although it is more common among Sunnis. Those who follow Sufism believe that they can achieve "oneness" with Allah by meditating, or exploring their inner thoughts, and by repeating **sacred** phrases, performing breathing exercises, dancing, and singing hymns. A spiritual leader known as a *shaykh* teaches Sufi students, or *murids*, how to perform these acts.

Muslim law

Islam is not only a set of religious beliefs. It is a set of laws, called the *Shari'ah*. The *Shari'ah* teaches people how to behave, helps them decide between right and wrong, sets out punishments for crimes, and explains how to deal with disputes between family members and other issues. The *Shari'ah* is based on the *Qur'an*, as well as the *Sunnah* and *Hadith*.

(above) Children learn the **Qur'an** from a very early age. Both boys and girls are taught by their parents. Some boys also go to religious schools where **mullahs** teach them how to read Arabic, the language of the **Qur'an**, and how to chant the verses of the **Qur'an**.

Mullahs

Each community has one or two *mullahs*, who are responsible for teaching the *Qur'an*, leading group prayers, and performing weddings, funerals, and other ceremonies. There are fewer *mullahs* in the countryside than in cities. In the countryside, *mullahs* often have other jobs such as farming. *Mullahs* are chosen by the government, which consults with each community. Being chosen a *mullah* is a great honor. Other important people in the Muslim community are the *muezzin*, who calls people to prayer from a mosque's **minarets**; the *qazi*, who is a religious judge responsible for administering the *Shari'ah*; and the *khadim*, who maintains and cleans the mosque.

(left) Muslims must remove their shoes and wash their hands, feet, and faces before entering a mosque.

Jihad and Taliban-style Islam

Jihad, which means "striving," is the responsibility of Muslims to strive to be good and to follow the teachings of Allah. Most Muslims believe that by leading a life based on Muslim teachings, they can show others the benefits of following Islam. Sometimes, the meaning of *jihad* is misinterpreted. **Fundamentalists** believe *jihad* gives them the right to spread their religion by waging war. For this reason, *jihad* is often translated as "holy war."

The Taliban had their own style of Islam. They interpreted the *Shari'ah* very strictly and introduced laws based on ancient tribal customs, such as forbidding women to work or own property or prohibiting people from playing games. Even though these laws went against the true teachings of Islam, people who criticized the Taliban were accused of being anti-Muslim.

Superstitions

In many parts of the countryside and in some cities, people combine Muslim beliefs with superstitions from times before Islam. For example, people believe that if they look at the moon on the third night after it is new, they will have bad luck. An itchy palm means they will receive money, and an itchy foot means they will go on a trip. If they bite their tongue, someone is talking about them behind their back. Many superstitions have to do with a belief in good and bad spirits that help or harm people. *Jinns* are demon-like creatures that hide in dark places, such as wells, and play tricks on people. Women and children often wear amulets and **talismans** to keep *jinns* from harming them. Some talismans are worn on necklaces, bracelets, and anklets. Others are hung inside and outside people's homes.

Talismans are often made by tying fruit, nuts, and other objects in rags. The bundles are attached to trees near homes or villages to protect people from jinns *and other dangers.*

Ramadan and *Eids*

Afghanistan's religious holidays are based on the Muslim calendar. The Muslim calendar is a lunar calendar, which means that it follows the cycles of the moon. Each new month begins when a full moon appears. North Americans use the solar calendar, which follows the cycles of the earth around the sun. A year according to the Muslim calendar is about ten days shorter than a year according to the solar calendar, so a holiday might be in December one year, in November a couple years later, and in October a few years after that.

Ramadan

During the ninth month of the Muslim year, people celebrate the most important festival, *Ramadan*. Muslims believe that it was during this month that Muhammad received Allah's teachings from the angel Jibril, or Gabriel. To celebrate the holy month, all people, except those who are old, sick, pregnant, or very young, fast from dawn to dusk every day. Fasting is believed to teach discipline and compassion for those who are less fortunate.

During *Ramadan*, families gather just before dawn for a meal called *sahari*. In Kabul, Afghanistan's capital, a cannon goes off to make sure everyone wakes up in time for the meal. No more food or drink is consumed until the evening meal of *iftar*. Afghans traditionally begin *iftar* by eating dates, raisins, or other fruit, and then they enjoy a large meal with tea.

Eid ul-Fitar

Eid ul-Fitar is a joyous celebration at the end of *Ramadan*. The festival, which means "breaking of the fast," lasts three days. People gather for enormous feasts, complete with teas, fruits, vegetables, nuts, meat, rice, and sweets, such as *noql*, which are sugared almonds. *Eid ul-Fitar* is also a fun time for children, who receive new clothing and other gifts. When the Taliban were in power, people celebrated *Eid ul-Fitar* in a very serious and formal way. Today, people are adding music to their celebrations, going to fairs, and gathering with family and friends.

Muslims gather outside the Great Mosque in Kabul after meeting for prayer during Ramadan. *Many Muslims wear special caps called* kufi *when they pray to show respect for Allah.*

Many cites in Afghanistan celebrate Eid ul-Fitar with fairs where people eat, play games and enjoy rides, such as this ferris wheel.

Eid ul-Adha

Eid ul-Adha marks the end of *hajj*, in the twelfth month of the lunar calendar. During the four-day celebration, people usually **sacrifice** a sheep. The meat is given to family members, neighbors, and poor members of the community as an act of *zakat*. The sacrifice of the sheep is a reminder of a story about the prophet Ibrahim, or Abraham. Allah asked Ibrahim to sacrifice his eldest son to prove his love for Allah. Just as Ibrahim was about to cut his son's throat, Allah told him to sacrifice a sheep instead.

Children crowd around a table filled with delicious desserts at an Eid ul-Fitar *celebration.*

Traditional festivals

Nazer are celebrations in which people give thanks for everything from recovering from an illness to returning home after a trip. *Nazer* celebrations also mark religious occasions, such as the anniversary of the birth and death of the prophet Muhammad. The festival, called *Mawlud Nabi*, can last for weeks, with people telling stories about Muhammad and his family.

Muharram

Muharram is a 40-day holiday that marks the brutal killing of Muhammad's grandson Hussain and male members of his family. It is celebrated mostly by Shias. The most important day of the festival is the tenth day, *Ashura*. This was the day on which Hussain was killed. On *Ashura*, men whip their backs with long chains that have small blades. The minor injuries that they suffer help them remember Hussain's suffering.

Young men from Kabul use chains to whip their chests and backs on the religious holiday of Ashura.

At Nauroz, people play soccer on the lawn outside the Roza Sharif Azarat Ali Shrine, in Mazar-e-Sharif.

Celebrating Nauroz

Although Afghanistan's religious holidays follow the Muslim lunar calendar, from day to day Muslims follow a version of the solar calendar called *shamsi*. According to *shamsi*, the new year begins on March 21, the first day of spring. *Nauroz*, or "new day," celebrates the first day of *shamsi*. People go on picnics, watch sporting events, or play games at fairs, where chickens and sheep dyed pink, green, purple, and yellow wander around the grounds. On *Nauroz*, people also celebrate the day that Ali, Muhammad's son-in-law and cousin, became the leader of Islam. They go on pilgrimages to the Blue Mosque, in the northern town of Mazar-e-Sharif, where they believe Ali is buried.

Thousands of people in Kabul crowd onto rooftops to watch a parade on Nauroz. For six years, Nauroz celebrations were forbidden by the Taliban.

Nauroz traditions

Eating delicious food is an important part of *Nauroz*. *Haft-mewah* is a cold soup made from walnuts, almonds, pistachios, red and green raisins, dried apricots, and *sanjid*, a date-like fruit. The seven fruits and nuts, which grow in spring, represent the new season. *Samanak* is a sweet pudding made of wheat that takes two days to prepare. *Jelabis* are deep-fried spirals of dough that are covered with syrup and molasses.

During *Nauroz*, some people perform **rituals**, such as jumping over bonfires, to rid themselves of illnesses. Many people, especially children, try to avoid an ugly old woman from legends named Ajuzak. It is said that Ajuzak walks around only on *Nauroz*, and that if she looks at a child, she will give him or her the evil eye, which is a curse. Other people believe that Ajuzak is a good spirit. Some farmers think that if it rains on *Nauroz*, it means that Ajuzak is home washing her hair and that the next year's **harvest** will be successful.

Zoroastrianism

Nauroz is based on the ancient religion of Zoroastrianism. Zoroastrians follow the teachings of Zoroaster, a religious scholar from **Persia** who lived between 625 and 551 B.C. His teachings are written in a holy book called the Avesta. According to Zoroastrianism, there is one god named Ahura Mazda. An evil spirit, Angra Mainyu, opposes Ahura Mazda and brings evil to the world. When the Taliban was in power, they banned *Nauroz* and the practice of Zoroastrianism because both were based on ideas that they considered contrary to Islam. Today, people are celebrating *Nauroz* again.

Jeshn

In August, Afghans celebrate *Jeshn*, a holiday that marks the end of Britain's rule over Afghanistan, in 1919. Britain had ruled the country off and on for more than 80 years. *Jeshn* also celebrates the harvest season. During the festivities, people listen to speeches by political leaders and watch parades, horse races, fireworks, and performances of the *atan*, Afghanistan's national dance.

Classmates rehearse for a Jeshn parade, in which they will perform a dance.

 # Sing and dance

For much of Afghanistan's history, people have used music and dance to express their religious faith. One of the earliest forms of religious music was *regvida*. *Regvida* songs were often about a person's devotion to Allah. The sounds, rhythms, and themes of *regvida* continue to influence Afghanistan's modern music.

Sufi music

People who practice Sufism play a distinct type of music that they believe helps them communicate with Allah. The haunting music is often played on a *rebab*, a stringed instrument with a very short neck and a metal **soundboard**. The *rebab* creates an echoing sound when its strings are plucked.

Folk music

Each **ethnic group** in Afghanistan has its own style of folk music, with its own sound. Regardless of where a song is from, it usually tells about honor, love, war, and family. Sometimes, the theme of love is disguised with references to roses and nightingales. Many folk songs are based on **epic poems** and folktales.

Landai, which are two-line poems set to music, are usually sung by Pashtun women. Pashtuns are the largest group of people in Afghanistan. The poems tell about daily life in Afghanistan, love, war, and politics. According to one popular story, the Afghan army was ready to retreat during a battle against the British in the 1800s. After a woman named Malalai sang them a *landai*, the Afghan army was inspired to keep fighting and won the battle.

Ghazals

Ghazals are a type of slow folk song based on Persian and Pashto poetry. Pashto is one of Afghanistan's main languages. Common themes in *ghazals* are love and one's devotion to Allah. *Ghazal* musicians play *rebabs*; *sarangis* and *delrubas*, which are stringed instruments played with bows; and *tablas* and *dhols*, which are drums. Some songs also use flutes and oboes, as well as a harp-like instrument called a *vaj*.

(top) Family members clap their hands and play along to a regvida *song at a wedding.*

Banned music

At one time, Afghans in large cities listened to radios playing music, news, and other programs over loudspeakers in the main streets. In 1992, a group known as the Mujahiddin, or "holy warriors," took control of parts of Afghanistan. Their goal was to spread Islam and restore the Muslim character of Afghanistan. They banned many types of music. Only songs that supported the Mujahiddin were encouraged. Musicians required a license from the government to perform, so many left the country.

When the Taliban came to power, it banned all music except for religious chants. People were not allowed to play music at weddings and other celebrations, and anyone found with a cassette tape or instrument was fined, beaten, or jailed. Even more musicians left the country. Today, some of these musicians are returning, while others remain in their new countries and sing about the hardships that Afghans face.

A man carefully takes his dhol out from under his house where he hid it during Taliban rule.

A man chooses a tape to purchase at a music store in Herat.

Popular music

Many Afghan musicians have become popular in Afghanistan and throughout the world. One of the best known musicians is Ahmad Zahir (1946–1979). He changed Afghan music by combining traditional melodies, instruments, and poetry with contemporary sounds. His songs were about traditional themes, such as love and one's relationship with Allah, but they were also about issues in Afghan society, especially politics. In his songs, he used instruments such as *tablas*, *rebabs*, and *dhols*, as well as guitars, saxophones, and accordions.

15

Traditional dance

Most dances in Afghanistan are performed at religious celebrations and ceremonies, or at special occasions such as weddings. Pashtuns traditionally danced the *atan* before heading out to war. Today, the *atan* is considered Afghanistan's national dance. Musicians play *dhols* and wind instruments called *surnai* while large groups of men carrying sticks, swords, or guns dance in circles, clapping, shouting, stamping, and twirling around. In another dance, men and women line up in rows of ten or twelve and dance while waving brightly colored scarves above their heads.

(right) Pashtun men dance the atan *during an* Eid ul-Fitar *celebration.*

(below) Afghan men, accompanied by musicians playing dhols, *dance at a* Nauroz *celebration.*

Time for fun

Many Afghan games are similar to games that North American children play. *Juz bazi* is like hopscotch, and *chishm putukan*, or "little eye hiding," is similar to tag. When one child spots another child hiding, he or she yells out, "*Mah!*"

Other games are unique to Afghanistan. *Akhamchai* is traditionally played by Hazara girls, who live in Hazarajat, a region in central Afghanistan. They form a circle, and then jump up and crouch down while singing one musical note at a time. The girls create different songs depending on the order in which they jump. *Buzul-bazi* is a game that is similar to dice, but it is played with a sheep's knucklebones. Children toss the bones, and whoever has the most bones standing upright gets the most points. Some children are not allowed to play *buzul-bazi* because people think that it is like gambling, which is forbidden.

Each Friday, these children meet at a playground in Kabul to fly kites.

Flying kites

Brightly colored kites flying through the skies were a rare sight during Taliban rule. Kite flying, which is one of Afghanistan's favorite pastimes, was against the law. Today, people are returning to parks and to streets to fly kites for fun and for kite fighting competitions. In these competitions, people coat their kite strings with a mixture of glass and glue and use the sharp strings to cut down other people's kites.

Men and boys playing turk'm jangee, *or "egg fighting," compete to see who can smash hard-boiled eggs the hardest without breaking them. They use many tricks to strengthen their eggs, such as filling the shells with cement.*

17

Buzkashi can be dangerous. Riders often fall off their horses because the animal's carcass is so heavy.

Buzkashi

Nomadic warriors from northern Afghanistan invented *buzkashi*, a sport played on horseback. *Buzkashi* is now played by many Afghans, especially by Uzbeks, Tajiks, and Turkmen, who live in the north.

There are several versions of *buzkashi*, which means "grab the goat." In one version, individual horseback riders try to grab the carcass, or headless body, of a goat or calf from a circle in the center of a playing field. They must ride with the carcass across a finish line that surrounds the field. In another version of *buzkashi*, two teams start at one end of the field; grab the carcass, which is in a circle on the field; ride around a flag at the opposite end of the field; then return to their starting point. In both versions, players must hold the carcass tightly to avoid dropping it or having others steal it from them.

Pahlwani

Pahlwani, which is similar to wrestling, is popular throughout Afghanistan, especially in major cities, where people watch competitions in clubs. The object of *pahlwani* is to knock down and hold down an opponent. Players cannot touch their opponents' legs, but they can grab their arms, bodies, or clothing. By the end of a match, competitors are often left wearing only shredded bits of fabric.

Pahlwani wrestlers test each other's strength before trying to throw one another off balance.

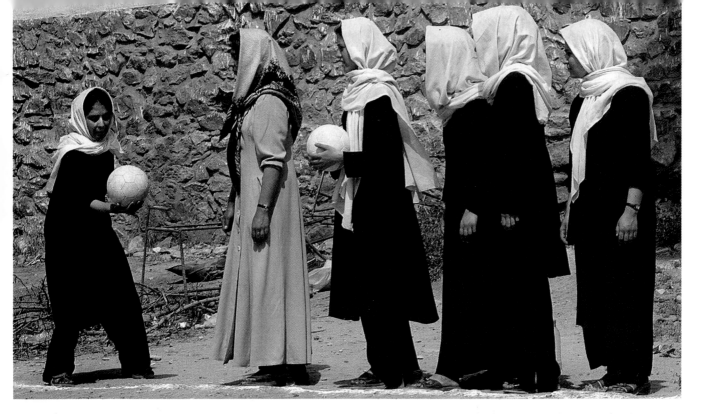

Hunting

Afghans hunt many animals, including birds, wild cats, goats, and sheep. They often use Afghan hounds, or *tazi*, to track their prey and retrieve it once it is dead. *Tazi* have long legs that allow them to run quickly, thin bodies that allow them to move and turn easily through difficult **terrain**, and an excellent sense of smell.

Burfi

To celebrate the first snowfall, many adults play a game called *burfi*. They put snow in envelopes, then try to leave the envelopes by their friends' front doors or porches without being caught. People who receive envelopes must throw parties for those who delivered them. If people are caught dropping off the letters, their foreheads are smeared with charcoal, and they must throw parties for the friends they tried to trick.

(above) Girls at a high school in Kabul learn how to serve, or hit, a volleyball during gym class.

(right) A rider moves in to pull a tent peg from the ground during a fast-paced game of naiza bazi *in Bamiyan.*

Naiza bazi

Naiza bazi, or "tent pegging," is a sport enjoyed mainly by Pashtuns. The game has its origins in tribal raids that took place more than 500 years ago. Riders on horseback use three-pronged **lances** to touch tent pegs stuck in the ground, to pull out the pegs, and to carry the pegs to different areas of a playing field. Team members get different numbers of points depending on what they do and how far they carry the tent pegs.

In this Gandhara sculpture, the Buddha has wavy hair like that of a Greek god. Wavy hair is often found in Gandhara art.

Gandhara art combines elements of ancient Roman, Greek, and Indian art. Paintings and sculptures of the Buddha are decorated with vines; angels; centaurs, which are mythical beings that are half man, half horse; and tritons, which are mythical beings that have the body of a man and the tail of a fish. These show the influence of Roman art. The Buddha himself wears long, flowing robes, which are similar to those worn by gods and goddesses in Greek styles of art. His face is painted or sculpted simply, and the jewelry he wears is quite plain, reflecting the influence of Indian art.

Gandhara sculptures

Among the best-known sculptures from the Gandhara era are "the Buddhas of Bamiyan," which once stood in the Bamiyan Valley, in the center of the country. The two enormous statues were carved out of sandstone cliffs, painted, and decorated with beautiful ornaments. In 2001, the Taliban, which set out to destroy all artwork that was not Muslim, almost completely destroyed the Buddhas.

Communities around the world are trying to help Afghanistan rebuild the Buddhas of Bamiyan.

Jewelry, coins, pottery, tools, and weapons from **civilizations** that ended thousands of years ago have been discovered throughout Afghanistan. Some of these **artifacts** come from settlements that date back to 100 000 B.C. Artifacts have also been found along the Silk Road, which was an ancient trade route that linked China and Rome. Many styles of art and ideas were passed from country to country, and from region to region within Afghanistan along this route.

Gandhara art

Gandhara art is a style of art whose main subject is the Buddha, the founder of **Buddhism**. Buddhism flourished from the first century B.C. to 600 A.D. in a region that included the eastern part of present-day Afghanistan and northwestern Pakistan.

A doorway at the Masjid-i-Jami, or Friday Mosque, in Herat, is decorated with tiles and panels on which calligraphers painted short passages from the Qu'ran. The panels are not only beautiful; they also remind people of their faith in Allah when they are not worshiping.

Muslim art

Many Muslim artists do not depict humans or animals in their work because they believe that only Allah has the power to create living things. Instead, they decorate buildings, jewelry, and pottery with intricate designs of leaves, flowers, and geometric shapes. They also write passages of the *Qur'an* using calligraphy, which is an elaborate form of writing. To draw the beautiful lettering, calligraphers dip brushes and pens with different-sized tips into ink or paint.

An intricate mosaic made up of a geometric border, flowers, and vines decorates the floor of a mosque. To make a mosaic, artists break large tiles into smaller pieces and then fit them together with plaster to make complicated designs.

Illuminations and miniatures

Beginning in the 1400s, artists illustrated poems and stories from folklore, history, and religion with small drawings and designs in the borders. People called them illuminated manuscripts because the gold and silver paint used to decorate them made the pages look shiny and bright. Artists also created miniatures. These small paintings showed scenes from Persian stories and poems in vibrant colors and great detail. The western city of Herat was the center of miniature painting in Afghanistan. Artists came from all over to perfect their skill there.

Modern art

Many of Afghanistan's artists were forced to flee the country during times of war. The sculptor Ahmanoolah Haiderzad left in 1979 and now lives in the United States. He designed Afghanistan's **emblem**, which appears on the country's flag and **currency**. Youssef Kohzad, an artist who founded the Kabul Museum, also moved to the United States. His paintings show scenes of life in Afghanistan before much of the country was destroyed by war.

The Kabul Museum

The Kabul Museum was once home to the largest collection of art and artifacts in Afghanistan. The Bagram Collection included more than 1,800 artifacts from ancient Rome, India, Greece, Egypt, and central Asia, and was the largest collection of Greek and Roman coins in the world. The museum also held one of the largest collections of pre-Islamic art and sculpture, including pieces from the Gandhara era. Many of the museum's collections were destroyed during years of war. Other pieces were stolen and sold to buyers around the world.

The Kabul Museum was closed in 1992 and bombed in 1993. Artifacts that survived were sealed in a vault in the basement or moved to other countries, such as Pakistan and India. In 2001, the Taliban passed a law that required all pre-Islamic art and artifacts to be destroyed. Many of the ancient relics that had been saved were demolished. The Kabul Museum remains closed, but people hope that it will reopen one day so they can learn about their country's rich artistic past.

A servant presents a parrot to an emperor in this illustration from a Persian folktale called Tutinamah, or Tales of a Parrot. During the 1400s and 1500s, many Persian stories were illustrated by Afghan artists.

Ancient architecture

Throughout Afghanistan, buildings with tall minarets, bulb-shaped domes, and colorfully painted tiles dot the landscape. Many are mosques and tombs built to honor religious figures and important Afghan heroes. The Blue Mosque, in Mazar-e-Sharif, has tiles that look like they are painted with flowers, but the floral patterns are actually made from tiles cut into different shapes and plastered together. The Kharka Sharif, in the southeastern city of Kandahar, is a shrine that holds a cloak believed to be the prophet Muhammad's. The cloak is carefully guarded within the shrine's thick walls, which are decorated with mosaics and verses from the *Qur'an*.

Once magnificent buildings

Many of Afghanistan's magnificent buildings now stand in ruins. Time, harsh weather, and war have damaged many historic sites. The Madjide Haji Pivada, in Balkh, was built in the 800s, making it one of the oldest mosques in the world. Decorative tiles still cling to its remaining walls and columns. The ancient complex of Sorkh Kowtal, in northeastern Afghanistan, includes the remains of two temples and a staircase that once linked a series of terraces.

The Minaret of Jam

The Minaret of Jam, which was built in 1194, stands on the southern bank of the Hari River, in western Afghanistan. The minaret, which is 71 feet (65 meters) tall, is made of bricks and is decorated with geometric patterns, flowers, and inscriptions in an ancient script called Kufic. Archaeologists disagree about why the minaret was built. Some believe it was part of a mosque, but no ruins of a mosque have been found at the site. Others believe it was built as a tower to mark a victory in battle. Today, archaeologists are uncovering ruins of a fortress, palace, wall with towers, cemetery, and **bazaar** on the northern bank of the river. They hope that these discoveries will give them more clues about the history of the area.

People come from hundreds of miles away to pray at the Blue Mosque in Mazar-e-Sharif.

In 2002, the United Nations Educational, Scientific, and Cultural Organization (UNESCO) added the Minaret of Jam to its World Heritage List and List of World Heritage in Danger. UNESCO wants to protect the intricate carvings from water damage and vandals.

Carpet weaving and other folk art

A woman weaves strips of colored wool on a loom to create a complicated carpet pattern.

Carpet patterns

Different tribes weave different patterns and symbols, called *gols*, into their carpets. Some patterns are made of geometric shapes, while others have images from nature, such as trees, birds, and animals. Often, a family has its own *gol* and its own way of making a carpet, which it keeps secret. Only family members know how to knot the threads and how many threads to use.

Depending on the size of the carpet, the thickness of the weave, and the details in the pattern, a carpet can take four or five people several months to finish.

Afghanistan's **artisans** are known for making beautiful gold and silver jewelry that is often decorated with passages from the *Qur'an* or with precious and semi-precious stones. Artisans in Kandahar, in the southeast, and Badakhshan, in the northeast, are famous for their copper pots, trays, and jugs. Weavers make cotton, wool, linen, and silk fabric which are used to make clothes and blankets. Embroiderers decorate the fabric with gold braiding, mirrors, shells, and stones.

Weaving carpets

Afghanistan's best known form of folk art is carpet weaving. Afghan carpets are famous for their high quality, interesting patterns, and bright colors. Making a carpet is a time-consuming task that requires a lot of patience and skill. First, wool from goats and sheep is dyed with vegetables and **minerals**. Then, small pieces of wool are pulled through a woven frame and tied into knots. Once the knots are tied, the carpetmaker clips the ends of the wool threads so that they are all the same length, and washes the carpet to remove excess dye. Some carpets are made on **looms** instead of by hand. The looms, which are small and light, are often used by nomadic peoples.

Types of carpets

Different regions also have their own styles of carpets. Traditional carpets from Herat are made from bright red wool that is bordered with green and accented with yellow flecks. Carpets from Meymaneh, in northern Afghanistan, are made from the wool of Karakul sheep, which is soft and durable. Turkmen rugs, or blood red rugs as they are called, are woven from wool that is dyed a deep shade of red. The rugs have patterns made from eight-sided shapes that are filled in with designs. A good Turkmen rug gets brighter over time. Turkmen women also weave rugs from silk. The silk comes from silkworms imported from India and China. Women wrap the silkworm eggs in cloths around their necks, keeping the eggs warm until they hatch.

Two women shopping for carpets at a market in Kabul wear chadris. Chadris are long cloak-like garments made from silk, cotton, or linen. Women were forced to wear chadris during Taliban rule, but today they can choose what to wear.

Languages, past and present

Walking through the streets of Afghanistan, you may hear people greet each other in Pashto or Dari, the country's two main languages. Pashto is the language of the Pashtuns. It is also the official language of the Afghan government. Dari is most commonly spoken by the Tajiks, Hazaras, and Aimak, who live in northern Afghanistan. It is also used by the government in addition to Pashto, and is the main language of business, education, and literature. Both Pashto and Dari are based on a Persian language called Avista, with words from the Arabic and Hindi languages added in.

Writing Pashto and Dari

Both Pashto and Dari are written using the Arabic alphabet. Special marks over certain letters indicate sounds that are in Pashto and Dari, but not Arabic. The chart below has words in Pashto and Dari written in the English alphabet to give you an idea of how to pronounce them.

English	Pashto	Dari
Hello.	*Salam.*	*Salam.*
Goodbye.	*Da khudai pa aman* or *Pa makha di sha.*	*Khuda hafiz.*
Thank you.	*Manana.*	*Tashakor.*
You're welcome.	*Manana.*	*Qubili tashakor nist.*
See you soon!	*Tar bia lidoo!*	*Bazmi binim!*

A girl in Bamiyan practices writing in Pashto.

Other languages

Afghans speak many languages other than Pashto or Dari depending on the region and their ethnic group. Some Tajiks speak Tajiki, a language from Tajikistan. Baluchi tribes, who live in the southern deserts, speak Baluchi, and Hazaras speak Hazaragi. Both Baluchi and Hazaragi are based on Persian. Many Afghans speak more than one language, especially nomadic peoples who must be able to communicate with people from different communities as they travel from place to place. Before Taliban rule, Afghans also learned other languages such as English, French, German, and Russian in school. Today, some schools and universities are offering classes in these languages again.

A boy learns to read both Pashto and Dari at an outdoor school in Khawaja Hasan, in the east. He reads from right to left, instead of left to right like English, because that is how the Arabic script of the two languages is written.

Friends chat outside a market in Kabul. People who speak more than one language usually communicate with each other in Dari.

Poetry and stories

Reciting poems and telling stories about love, history, and heroes have been important parts of life in Afghanistan for thousands of years. Minstrels, called *sazinda* or *mutrib*, traveled from village to village, entertaining people with their poems, songs, and tales. Rulers kept poets and storytellers in their courts. The emperor Mahmud, who ruled Afghanistan and parts of Persia in the late 900s, had 400 poets in his court, including Firdausi. Firdausi (934–1020) was a Persian poet who wrote the epic poem *Shah-nama*, or *Book of Kings*, for Mahmud. *Shah-nama* told about Persia's glorious past.

Poets

Rabia Balkhi was a princess who lived in Balkh in the 800s. She was the first woman to write and recite poetry in Persian. She killed herself after her brother forbade her from marrying the slave she loved. She wrote her final poem in her own blood. Mowlana Jalaluddin Rumi (1207–1273) wrote poems about his love for Allah. His belief in Sufism greatly influenced his work.

Two of Afghanistan's most famous poets emerged during the 1600s. Khushal Khan Khattak (1613–1689) is Afghanistan's national poet. He was a warrior, writer, and leader of the Khattak tribe of Pashtuns. Many of Khattak's poems describe the struggles of the Afghan people or tell of bravery, honor, love, and appreciating life. Khattak also wrote books on **philosophy**, medicine, and **ethics**, as well as an autobiography, or book about his life. Abdul Rahman (1633–1715) wrote two volumes of poems with simple messages about religion and life in Afghanistan. He was so well loved by the Afghan people that he was nicknamed "Baba," which means "Grandfather."

Many stories in Shah-nama *tell of Alexander the Great, who invaded present-day Afghanistan from 329 to 326 B.C. In this illustration Alexander slays a terrifying dragon.*

Poetry today

Whether today's authors write novels, short stories, or plays, they almost always write poetry too. Common themes in poetry include war, love, jealousy, religion, and folklore. One of the most popular modern poets is Khalilullah Khalli (1907–1987). He is known for his poetry collection *Matumserai*, or *The House of Waiting*, which deals with the troubles of Afghanistan and its people. Khalli left Afghanistan in 1978 and lived in a **refugee** camp in Pakistan until his death.

Journalist Latif Pedram is a well known Afghan poet and political activist, or person who fights for political change. When the Taliban came into power in 1996, he spoke out against them and was forced to leave the country in 1998. Today, he lives in France where he continues to write and speak out for the rights of all Afghans.

Stories for older children

Many children's stories have recurring characters, or characters who appear in book after book. One example is Bachey Kul, or "Bald Boy," who is a troublemaker with no hair. He always gets his way even though he is not very smart. In one story, Bachey Kul's brothers refuse to give him any of their parents' **inheritance**, so he sets out on a journey to find his fortune. During his travels, he meets many enemies, whom he tricks. In the end, he marries a beautiful princess and lives happily ever after in a huge palace — much wealthier than his brothers.

Another popular character is Mullah Nasrudin, who outsmarts everyone he speaks to. In one popular story, Nasrudin hangs a sign above a booth that tells people he will answer two questions for 100 silver coins. A person approaches the booth and asks, "Don't you think that 100 silver coins is quite expensive for only two questions?" Nasrudin replies, "Yes. Do you have a second question?"

Other stories

Kalilah wa Dimnah is a collection of fables about animals enjoyed by many people in Afghanistan. The stories were originally from India, but today children read them in Pashto or Dari.

The most popular Afghan legend is the story of Leila and Majnun. A poet named Quais bin Amir falls in love with Leila, the daughter of a nomadic chief, but his love for her is so great that he loses his mind. He is nicknamed "Majnun," which means "Mad One," because of his illness. Majnun realizes that he cannot marry Leila because he is mad, so he runs away. While searching for Majnun, Leila is put in prison by a prince, Ibn Salam, who wants to marry her. Leila escapes and finds Majnun, who explains to Leila why he cannot marry her. Filled with sorrow, Leila runs away and dies. When Majnun finds out what has happened to Leila, his heart breaks and he dies embracing her tombstone.

An Afghan tale

Many stories from Afghanistan tell of an *amir*, or king, who disguises himself to find out how his subjects live. In this story, an *amir* learns a valuable lesson from the people he observes.

The *amir* who became a weaver

Once there was a powerful *amir* and his *vizir*, or advisor, who disguised themselves as merchants and went to a *chaukhara*, or tea house, for a cup of spicy *chai* tea. As they sipped their tea, they overheard a conversation between two merchants.

"I wish the *amir* all of Allah's blessings, but I worry that he has no trade other than that of being an *amir*," the first merchant said. "I agree," added the second merchant. "Think of how boring his life must be. Day after day, all he does is meet with the Council, manage the State, and feast with foreign leaders."

The *amir* thought about what the merchants said and decided they were right. "Every person — even an *amir* — should have a trade in case it is needed one day. My loyal *vizir*, summon to the palace the land's greatest craftspeople so I can choose one of their trades to learn."

The next day, the *amir* watched as all the artisans worked. He was most impressed by a weaver who wove beautiful fabric, and decided that was the trade he would learn.

Eventually, the *amir* designed a pattern that he was very fond of. He wove a silk handkerchief with this pattern on it, and gave it to the queen.

Many months later, the *amir* and *vizir* were walking through the streets of the city disguised yet again. Two men attacked them, dragged them to a nearby house, and tied them up.

When the robbers found two pouches of gold coins in the sacks the *amir* and *vizir* were carrying, they laughed, "Now we can kill these two men and buy ourselves new clothes and lots of food!"

"Please do not harm us," pleaded the *amir*. "We are only two weavers from a small village."

"If you spare our lives," the *vizir* added quickly, "we can make you even wealthier. My friend can weave you the finest handkerchief worth 1,000 gold coins. That's nearly ten times the number of coins in those sacks."

The greedy robbers untied the *amir* and set him to work weaving a handkerchief. When the *amir* was done, the *vizir* suggested, "That is the finest handkerchief my friend has ever made. It is worthy of the queen herself. Take it to the palace. You will easily receive 1,000 gold coins for it."

So, one of the robbers set off to the palace and offered the handkerchief to the queen. She immediately recognized the pattern, and gave the messenger the gold coins he requested. As soon as he left, she turned to the royal spy and ordered, "Take some soldiers and follow that messenger. He will lead you to the *amir* and *vizir*."

The royal spy and the soldiers watched as the robber returned to the house where the *amir* and *vizir* were being held captive. They saw the robber grab the *amir* and command him to weave more handkerchiefs. "Once we have our fortune, we will kill you," they sneered.

Just as the *amir* began to weave his second handkerchief, the spy and the soldiers burst through the door and saved the *amir* and *vizir*. The robbers were thrown in prison for the rest of their lives, and the *amir* was reunited with the queen. "Thank Allah that you are so clever," he said. "And thank Allah that you learned a trade," she replied.

Glossary

amulet A charm worn to protect against evil

artifact A product, usually historical, made by human craft

artisan A skilled craftsperson

bazaar An area of small shops and stalls

Buddhism A religion that teaches that people are reincarnated, or born again after they die, and that behaving well in one life will ensure happiness in the next

civilization A society with a well-established culture that has existed for a long time

currency Money

descendant A person who can trace his or her family roots to a certain family or group

emblem An object or design used as a symbol

epic poem A long poem that tells of heroic deeds

ethics A set of moral principles or values

ethnic group A group of people who share a common race, language, religion, and history

fast To stop eating food or certain kinds of food for religious or health reasons

fundamentalist A person who follows a strict set of religious principles

harvest The gathering of crops

inheritance Money left after someone dies

invader A person who enters using force

lance A long wooden pole with a sharp iron or steel head

loom A machine used to weave strands of thread together to make cloth

minaret A tall, slender tower from which a crier calls Muslims to prayer

mineral A naturally occurring, non-living substance obtained through mining

mosque A Muslim house of worship

mystical Having spiritual meaning

nomadic Having no fixed home and moving from place to place in search of food and water

Persia The present-day country of Iran, to the west of Afghanistan

philosophy The investigation and study of human beliefs and wisdom

pilgrimage A religious journey to a sacred place

prophet A person who is believed to speak on behalf of God

refugee A person who leaves his or her home or country because of danger

ritual A religious ceremony in which steps must be followed in a certain order

sacred Having special religious significance

sacrifice To offer to God

shrine A small area or structure dedicated to a god or saint

soundboard Part of a musical instrument that enhances its sound

successor A person who takes the place of someone else

talisman An object that protects from evil and brings good fortune

terrain An area of land

Index

1 2 3 4 5 6 7 8 9 0   Printed in the USA   0 9 8 7 6 5 4 3